DON'T LEAVE IT ALL TO THE TEACHERS

PARENTING AND SCHOOLING

Dr Dean Alleyne EdD

Copyright © 2014 by Dr Dean Alleyne EdD

DON'T LEAVE IT ALL TO THE TEACHERS
PARENTING AND SCHOOLING
by Dr Dean Alleyne EdD

Printed in the United States of America

ISBN 9781498403405

All rights reserved solely by the author. The author guarantees all contents are original and do not infringe upon the legal rights of any other person or work. No part of this book may be reproduced in any form without the permission of the author. The views expressed in this book are not necessarily those of the publisher.

Cover Image © Dean Alleyne
dalleyne20@hotmail.ca

Edited by Xulon Press

www.xulonpress.com

[signature]
19/11/2016

I hope the contents help you assist your child in its journey through school.

TABLE OF CONTENTS

Introduction vii

Chapter 1: Things You Can Do At Home To Help Your Child Succeed. 11

Chapter 2: Preparing For The Transfer From Elementary To Junior High School 15

Chapter 3: Grade Seven: First Year In Junior High School 23

Chapter 4: Grade Eight: Perhaps The Most Vulnerable Year. 29

Chapter 5: Grade Nine: The Year For Major Decisions . . 35

Chapter 6: Grades Ten, Eleven And Twelve. 39

Chapter 7: The Months Leading Up To The Finals. 43

Chapter 8: How To Get The Most Out Of A Parent-Teacher Interview 47

Chapter 9:   Homework Scenarios And Some
             Suggestions For Parents 53

Chapter 10: Helping Your Child Cope With
             The Stress Of Homework. 61

Chapter 11: Class Work, Homework
             And Teacher Expectation 65

Chapter 12: Parenting Style And Classroom Practice 69

Chapter 13: Helping Your Child Make Decisions 73

Chapter 14: How To Help Your Child Using Motivation . . .79

Chapter 15: How Family Values Can Influence
             Schooling 83

Chapter 16: Some Tips On How To Deal With
             Parent-Child Conflict. 87

Chapter 17: How To Be A Positive Parental
             Role Model. 89

Bibliography. 93

Introduction

This book aims to take parents into their child's learning environment without the stress, which some parents have, of schools and teacher particularly when they have to meet the teachers. It sets out to show them some key aspects of schooling, which can have a lasting effect on the outcome of a child's education and life chances. I do not claim to have all the answers, nor do I intend to lecture to parents on how to bring up their children. I merely set out to provide parents with some of the tools and skills that will enable them to enhance their children's chances of succeeding at secondary school.

In my professional capacity as a teacher for thirty-two years, and finishing my career as a principal, I experienced situations where parents, through the lack of information and an understanding of how schools work, were ill-equipped to help their children as much as they wanted to. This, more than anything else, was the driving force behind the writing of this book. The suggestions put forward can be applied across all ethnic groups.

I have been able to observe many of the reasons for under-achievement played out firsthand. I have also observed many students, with the potential to do well, just simply fold up and fail to register any significant level of achievement at the end of their school career. I, therefore, felt the time had come to research the experiences of a group of successful students and their families, and share the findings with other families in a manner that would assist them to better understand how the education system works, and what they can do to enable their children to navigate the system and achieve the best from it. The book is, therefore, aimed at parents and is meant to be a practical aid in helping their children to reach a provincially acceptable level of achievement.

Many parents, in recognizing the dilemma, have often asked me what can be done to help their children to do better. The fact is that although they were able to *recognize* the dilemma, they had no way of addressing the situation in a manner to bring about a *realization* of success. This is because although you may recognize the problem, without the essential *realization tools,* you will not be able to enhance your child's chances of high achievement. It is here I felt there was no better way for me to put something back into the system than offering some practical advice to parents on how to recognize situations, and how to acquire and use realization tools: in short, to provide them with a toolkit.

Often, when parents are asked how they get involved in their children's education, most tend to say by attending parent-teacher interviews or consultation evenings and seeing that homework is done. While this is to be applauded, and in most cases is enough to see some children successfully through high school, there is evidence to show that it is certainly

Introduction

not so for many others, including those for whom English is a second language. It was clear to me during my research that such families had to be taken beyond the level of parent-teacher interviews and homework sessions. I hope that by the time you have read this book, you are better equipped to facilitate your child's progress through the secondary system. It aims to get disengaged parents engaged, and those already engaged to become even more engaged.

The book is written in a style that makes it easily accessible. Each topic ends with a list of suggestions you will find useful. It is set out in a manner that allows you to accompany your child from grade seven to twelve. The value of the book is that, once read, it can be used as a companion guide during the entire school career of your child. It will enable you to help your child navigate the system and realize their potential. It is not meant to be a blueprint to success, but an aid to success.

Chapter One

Things You Can Do At Home To Help Your Child Succeed.

Some general tips

There is much research to show that children whose parents get *actively* involved in their schooling tend to do better. My experience has led me to conclude that while some parents have a desire to get more involved in their children's education, they don't know how to go about it. One reason given by parents is that schools have changed very much since they were students. Curriculum changes, like subject matter and teaching methods, may be unclear to them. However, if you accept that learning is the road to success, then as a parent, it is worth your while investing some time in your child's schooling. In other words, it is worth getting more engaged.

Suggestions
- If you had any bad experiences about your school days, avoid sharing them with your child, particularly when they are about to move from the primary

to the secondary sector. This could give him/her the wrong impression about school. Instead, tell your child about the **pleasant and interesting** times you had. Always demonstrate a positive attitude about school to your child.

- Make a point of talking to them about what they are doing at school. This tells the youngster you are genuinely interested in what he or she is doing. It will also give you a chance to share any knowledge you have with them.
- Provide a corner where they can study quietly away from TV or any other external distractions.
- Decide with your child a good time to do homework and stick to it as closely as possible. Some children like to get it done and out of the way as soon as they get home. Others need a break to unwind before starting.
- Always ask what homework or assignment has been given and look it over when finished. Try to **avoid excessive nagging**. The aim is for the young student to learn to organize their time to ensure the work gets done.
- If homework isn't getting done, talk to the teacher about the kind of help your child may need. Remember that **working together with the teacher** is in the best interest of the student. (More about homework in chapter 9)
- Make a point of talking to your child almost every night. Studies have shown that children whose parents do so tend to do better in school than children whose parents

Things You Can Do At Home To Help Your Child Succeed.

hardly talk to them except to argue. Try to **eat one meal seated together every day if possible and talk** about what's going on in everyone's life *without arguing.*

Chapter Two

Preparing For The Transfer From Elementary To Junior High School

Moving from elementary to junior high is more than moving from one place to another. It also means moving from a state of childhood to one of adolescence, with all its physical and emotional changes. It is therefore one of the key stages in a child's life when both internal and external changes may be taking place.

Why is preparation necessary?
- Entering the world of the junior high school can be a daunting experience for an eleven or twelve-year-old. Yesterday the youngster was at the top of their elementary school, today they find themselves at the bottom in a new, and perhaps larger, world.
- They were once in a class, perhaps assigned to one room and may be taught by no more than two teachers,

now they have to move from room to room and be taught by several teachers.
- In the elementary school, teaching was more pupil-based rather than subject-based. It was a place where teaching and learning took place in an environment that provided a sense of security that can be immediately lost on entry junior high.
- In elementary school, the young student had a room, a base in which all their belongings were kept, now he/she is expected to exercise greater responsibility. They must become more organized and be ready to take the appropriate equipment with them to the next lesson.
- They may even be overcome by sheer numbers of students and staff milling around, leaving them in a state of confusion and fear in their new world. Such can be the initial experience of the newcomer to the world of the high school. This may be the world that awaits them.

How to first prepare yourself for the transfer.
- Whatever fears and anxieties you may have about the move to junior high, be sure not to pass them on to your child. Instead, talk about the excitement of moving to a new school and discuss any concerns your child might have. You must **be positive and upbeat about the move**.
- It may also be a difficult time for you. After all, you are now seeing your child move on to a new phase in their development, a situation that may cause you great concern about how they will get on with others and how

well he or she will settle into their new environment. You must therefore **be prepared to chat very often with them** about what they are doing at school and show a genuine interest in their new friends.

- **Be prepared for the unexpected**. For example, the change could cause your child to become very anxious and stressed. This can express itself in the form of unusual childish behavior, tears and tantrums, or not wanting to go to school. This is one of the reasons why you must talk to the child very often about school.
- **Be prepared to be vigilant.** Don't assume that because your child might have done well in elementary school that they will automatically do equally well from the start in junior high. Look out for any unusual behavior that may arise from the work being too overwhelming or even boring. If they complain constantly about boring work, it might be that it is not sufficiently challenging. Time for you to intervene. Get in touch with the school to have the problem addressed. They may even be finding it hard to make new friends. Whatever the problem, have it addressed as soon as possible. Not to do so may find your child playing truant or refusing to attend school.
- You will probably be invited to the new school before your child starts. Be prepared to **find out some or all of the teachers likely to teach your child in the first year and have an informal chat.**

What are the benefits?
   a) This helps to build a rapport between teacher, you and the child.
   b) It gives you an opportunity to find out what will be covered in the first year. You will then have a chance to give the child a head start by doing some reading ahead or providing help with the basics in the core subjects.
   c) This will tell the teacher that you are interested in your child's schooling and are prepared to do whatever it takes to support their learning.
   d) It will also tell the child you are very interested in their education and that they can depend on your active support.
   e) All of this will help to boost your child's self-confidence, a characteristic they will need throughout school and beyond.
   f) By helping your child, you are indirectly helping the teacher to help your child.

Your duty as a parent, therefore, is to ensure that your child's emotional well being and development are safeguarded as they move on to junior high. The ease with which your child settles in is therefore directly related to **how you and the young student are prepared for that transition**. You owe it to your child to make that transition a pleasant and positive experience. Some schools do have a scheme whereby new students are invited for a day or half a day to be shown around and learn a bit about the geography of the school. This is positive, but parents ought to be aware that more is needed on their part to make the transfer as smooth as possible.

How to prepare your child for the transfer
Here are four of the common concerns children have:
Bullying: Will I be bullied by older pupils?
Getting lost: My new school is so large, what if I get lost!
The work: Will I be able to keep up with school work?
New friends: Will I be able to make new friends?

- During the last year in elementary school, get your child to talk about those things in which they are interested. These may include subjects taught in the classroom as well as out-of-school activities. Encourage them to share their feelings with you. This tells them you are interested in what they are doing and that **they can depend on your support in the future**.
- Although the elementary school might have taken them to museums and other places of interest, try to take them to these and other places yourself, but make sure you get them to **write about what they learned from the visit and to talk about it**. This broadens their knowledge base and teaches them to express themselves, all of which can boost their confidence. Always remember that nothing gives a newcomer more excitement than being able to chat to friends about places they visited and things they learned.
- During the summer break prior to starting at junior high, use the computer and whatever means you can

to **provide them with a head start**, even the help of an older sibling or a friend of the family, if you do not feel confident enough to do so yourself. Be careful not to overwork the youngster who must still have time to enjoy their last long break before starting at their new school.

- About a week or two before starting at the new school, **encourage your child to go to bed a bit earlier**. This helps to prepare them for the new regime they will be facing.
- Try to avoid older siblings filling your child's head with mythical stories of what might happen when they arrive at junior high. Reassure them they will be looked after and that any worries will be shared.
- For most children, it might mean a break-up of a friendship group, but this can sometimes be an opportunity to break some of those unhealthy alliances that might have developed at elementary school.

Preparing your child for racist encounters

As children develop, they become more exposed to race-related contacts, comments and conversations, the content of the TV, film and printed material through which they incorporate cultural messages about the relevance of race. It is in the middle years of school that the dialogue with parents about race assumes enormous importance. Racism is an unfortunate fact of life that can bring out strong emotions. It is therefore essential to have a strong coping strategy you can teach your child, so here are a few suggestions.

Suggestions
- From an early age, set the right example by keeping your children well-informed about the different cultures. Talk to them about the effects of prejudice against race, disability, age, religion, and sex. Point out that they should all be respected even if hard to understand.
- Teach them to know their worth about their cultural background and how to be proud of it. Get them to research well-known personalities in their heritage. Discuss the influence of such personalities and the part they played to make you feel proud of your cultural background. Let them know not to accept racial stereotypes and not to lose their identity.
- Try to develop and encourage an open dialogue with your child and encourage them to discuss any problem.
- Let them know they can do anything they set their minds on and not to accept any different. Get them to understand not to allow where they come from determine where they can go.
- It is important that your children see you having friendships with people of different cultures so that they can begin to understand how they can relate to each other.
- By providing them with honest information and guidance and helping them to focus on the good side of things, like doing all it takes to succeed, you will be giving them that extra strength to deal with racist incidents.

Chapter Three

Grade Seven: First Year In Junior High School

Making Friends

Some children are fortunate enough to be going to the same junior high school or to be placed in the same group as some of their friends from elementary school. This gives them a feeling of security in that they tend to support each other. But from time to time they have to make new friends, and this is where parents tend to get very anxious. Although you cannot ultimately make such choices for them, you ought to be able to provide them with certain guidelines.

Suggestions:
- **Try to make sure your child knows what the family stands for: its family values, the framework within which the family operates.** Some families tend to draw on religious or other philosophical principles. If this has been part of the child's upbringing from a very early age, then there should not be much of a

problem getting them to understand the link between such values, schooling, and the importance of making the right choice of friends. Remember that, as individuals, we make decisions against a background of experience, be it first or second hand. Children do so against a background of family values transferred to them through daily experiences.

- Make an effort to find out **the value placed on education by the family** of any boy or girl with whom your child may choose to be friends. It is not the best start to have your child be constantly in close contact with another youngster who is anti-school, anti-social and anti-authority. Such a youngster often has a strong personality, one strong enough to overpower most children of their age. The last thing you want is to have your child come under such negative influences.

- It is often said that 'like-things attract like-things.' Once your child has a good reserve of family values to draw on, he/she will use these to help them make their choices. They will seek out friends who want to do well, who want their parents to be proud of them and who want to be proud of themselves. In short, they will seek out friends of **similar background and thinking**.

- If you are satisfied with their choice of friends, then it can be helpful to liaise with those families for joint ventures like going to places of interest or arranging joint homework sessions on Saturdays, etc. It can also be a forum for discussing issues of concern as well as the good things happening at school.

- Most children in the first year have a very short concentration span, probably about five minutes. As a parent, you therefore have to stress the need and importance of **listening** to what the teacher is saying. Impress upon your child that, in order to **understand,** they must first listen. It is an exercise you can do at home to increase their concentration span.
- Explain the benefits they can have from being **polite to others,** including teachers. If this is part of their upbringing, then it should not be difficult for them to take the same characteristic to school. It pays good dividends in that it could make life a lot easier for your child.
- Point out that there is a satisfactory way of handling differences between themselves and others, including teachers. Always remember, too, that your child will note the manner in which you handle differences at home and will assume that your way is the right way and therefore take it to school.
- Since a child absorbs what they see and hear at home in terms of behavior and take it to school, then please make sure that what they take to the classroom is the kind of family behavior you are happy to have exhibited.

Dealing with an incident in which your child is involved

When children are young, the way parents show their concern over negative incidents is important to building confidence. It can also provide evidence of support for children's desire for fair play and equal treatment. Here are some useful tips when an incident occurs involving your son or daughter.

Suggestions
- Listen *closely and sympathetically* to the child's account of the incident. Try to determine who was involved and who witnessed the incident. Get your child to *write down their version of the incident.*
- Give the child a notion of what you plan to do.
- As soon as possible, bring the incident to the attention of those in authority (teachers, administrators, parents) and engage in a discussion on the matter. Do not approach the matter with the notion that '*I am right*' and '*you are wrong.*' That does not help.
- Try to reach an agreement on what action will follow to influence behavior, interaction, policy and practice. Inform the child of your action on their behalf and suggest what must be done if it happens again.

CHAPTER FOUR

GRADE EIGHT: PERHAPS THE MOST VULNERABLE YEAR

My experience and my research suggest that if a child is going to become anti-school, the first signs are usually shown in the second year in junior high. In the first year, the young student was kept fully occupied:

- (a) trying to get off to a good start;
- (b) learning the geography of the school;
- (c) trying to impress his teachers;
- (d) making new friends;
- (e) making sure he impresses his parents;
- (f) probably getting lost.

However, as a parent, you must *not assume* that, because your son or daughter might have finished the first year successfully, he/she will be equally successful in the second year and beyond. By the time they reach the second year, they would have settled into a friendship group, be able to find their way around, and are no longer put off by the masses of students and teachers milling around them. They may even have developed a rapport with some of their favorite teachers.

Nevertheless, you have to be very vigilant. If the school has a system of testing or assessing during or at the end of the year, this is to your child's advantage. It gives them something on which to focus, making it less likely for them to be influenced by undesirable peers. If such a system is not part of the school curriculum, then there is always a chance that a number of things could happen, causing alarm bells to ring, so be very vigilant.

- The young student could see the second year as less important and put less effort into their work.
- The slack that is created could then be invaded by undesirable peer-group influences which, if not detected in time, could lead to the development of an anti-school, anti-authority and anti-progress attitude.
- With a reducing work-rate and a breakdown in classroom behavior, there is a likelihood of detentions and probable exclusion.

But horrendous as this may seem, there are steps that you, as a parent, can take to reduce the chances of that happening to your child.

Suggestions:
- Keep reminding your child that they are loved by the family. **Keep talking to them about the family values**

and the importance you place on a good education, whatever form it may take. Your child will need these values and reserves to draw on when faced with unwanted peer-group influences.

- Every evening, **make it a point of asking them about their day at school**. Find out what they thought were the good parts and the bad parts of the day and why. It will show them you have a keen interest in what they are doing. Keep a close eye on their homework. For instance:

    (a) See to it that homework is started every evening at the agreed time.
    (b) Never accept excuses from your child for not doing homework, *always investigate.*
    (c) Have a close look at any completed pieces of homework for quality and presentation.
    (d) Check that all pieces of work have been marked and pay close attention to the teachers' comments.

- Although there may be a parent-teacher interview, try if possible to speak to some of their course/subject teachers either in person or by email to find out if there are any problems arising like classroom work-rate. The idea is to nip things in the bud before they get out of hand. It also shows the teacher that you are engaged in your child's schooling.

- Be on the lookout for any distinct change in behavior like a drop in the dress code of the school or even the desire to hurry up homework in order to play electronic games or watch TV. If dissatisfied, seek help.
- But praise your child when he/she is doing well and ask them why they think they are doing well in that course or subject. Encourage them to transfer that attitude and approach to weaker areas.
- Your duty is to help your child stay focused, therefore continue to take them to places of interest and places they would like to visit. You may even encourage them to do a small project on something in which they are interested, but make sure their teacher sees it when finished.
- Encourage your child to spend some time on weekends and certainly during the school holidays reviewing what they did that week or term. Discuss with them any difficulties they are having and encourage them to read ahead.
- Where possible, both parents ought to attend the parents-teacher interview. This sends a strong message to the school and to your child:

    (a) It tells the school that you are **both** interested in the child's schooling. This helps to raise the teacher's expectation.

    (b) It tells the child that they have **the support of both parents**. This helps him/her to build confidence and stay on track.

Grade Eight: Perhaps The Most Vulnerable Year

Since, as stated earlier, most children who rebel and become anti-school tend to show signs in the second year, your task as a parent is to help them navigate their way through what may be the rough waters of that year.

CHAPTER FIVE

GRADE NINE: THE YEAR FOR MAJOR DECISIONS

The third year is a central year. It is the year that may require your child to make a number of major decisions of which the most significant is the *choice of courses or programs to follow in senior high. He or she must make sure that their selection meets the requirements of the college or* university that they may eventually want to attend. The choices made will affect how he or she spends their time at school for the next four years. It is also important to note that since your child's strengths, interests and career dreams will influence the courses they choose in junior and senior high school, you ought to work closely with teachers, school counselors and administrators to help your child move toward their future goal. Whether your child is thinking in terms of an apprenticeship, planning for college or considering going to university, here are some suggestions which as a parent you may want to take on board.

Suggestions:

- As your child approaches the end of grade eight or as early as possible in grade nine, make them understand that teachers prefer to have on their courses those students who show the potential to do well. Although this is something they may already know, there is no harm in emphasizing it.
- Talk to your child about the importance of having a **good education**. Talk about careers you find interesting and about the possibilities open to them with a good education. Point out that they ought not to allow where they come from to determine where they can go
- Explain that they are now at a major set of crossroads and that grade nine is the time for redoubling their effort. Point out that it is now highly likely they will be going in a direction different to that of their friends. Impress upon them that they should choose a program or course because they like it, because they find it interesting and believe strongly they can do well in it and *not* because their friend wants to do it.
- After choosing their courses, there is the summer break before starting senior high school. Get your child to use this period to their advantage. It can be used to get some groundwork done in some subjects. Try to find out what will be covered in grade ten and encourage them to do some advance reading. He/she can even spend some time strengthening those areas in core subjects like mathematics, English and science, where they may be a bit weak.

Grade Nine: The Year For Major Decisions

- During the summer holidays, it might be a good idea to arrange for your child to visit a place connected with what he or she would like to do in senior high. Perhaps a friend, a relative or work colleague may be helpful here. The school may also be able to assist you here. Such a visit could inspire the young student by helping them to firm up their goals and therefore sustain motivation. Even if they change their mind later, it doesn't matter. What matters is that they would have been kept focused all the while.

These are some of the ways you can help your child to have a foundation on which to launch their senior high school career. It is a way of getting them into the correct right mind-set. It is a way of giving that child a head-start that only pays good dividends.

CHAPTER SIX

GRADES TEN, ELEVEN AND TWELVE.

At this stage you will find your child has to do a lot more homework. They will already be feeling the pressure exerted on them from the expectations of you their parents, their teachers, the expectations of their peer-friends and, believe it or not, their own expectations. If all these expectations are roughly similar, then there is no problem. The fact is, however, it is hardly ever so and therefore the mind of that student suddenly becomes a battleground as to whose expectations ought to be satisfied. It can be very stressful, especially for a youngster who may also have the added stress of physical and emotional development, which can sometimes cause them to rebel in their effort to assert their autonomy. This is a situation that can cause much parent-child conflict. (refer to *Chapter 16 for some suggestions on how to deal with parent-child conflict*) Fortunately, most students tend to handle this quite well, but many others, however, need that extra input from parents in order to do so. Always remember your child, consciously or subconsciously, may be looking to you for help and guidance through this period. Supporting their learning at that time can assist them in achieving their objectives.

Suggestions:

- Whether or not you were giving your child the necessary support, now is the time to give them all the help you can. **Avoid negative comments and criticisms.** They don't help, they only dampen their confidence.
- **Show appreciation for the effort he/she is making** by giving them the occasional treat. Take them to a favorite place of their choice, but tell them why you are doing it. This can provide a chance for both of you to have a nice, friendly chat about any concerns. It also allows you a chance to praise him or her for the good work they are doing and to suggest how they may be able to do even better. At the same time, you may be able to discuss what can be done to improve any areas of weakness.
- **Help them manage their time.** This applies mainly to weekends. Come to an arrangement that will allow a fair balance between study and leisure time, and make sure that your child sticks to it. It is a kind of self-discipline. If all assignments have been completed, encourage them to spend some time reading ahead. It is good practice.
- **If your child is the sporting type, do not prohibit them.** Instead, help them to strike an appropriate balance between sports and academic work. Research

has shown that very often, students who are good at some kind of sport usually do very well academically. It is the case of 'a healthy mind in a healthy body.'
- As a parent, you can also **lead by example.** For instance, you may wish to plan a distance learning course in something however simple. You may then be able to plan your study time to coincide with theirs, especially on weekends. If possible, it may also be a good idea for both of you to study in the same room. You may just decide to read. You are there to help. You are there to encourage and what better way of doing so!
- Always **keep lines of communication open.** From time to time, talk to them about their strengths and their weaknesses and what can be done to help them where they are weak. If extra help is needed that you yourself might not be qualified to handle, then do all you can to provide that help, whatever form it takes.

If project work is part of the course, it can sometimes bring about untold stress to both student and parent if not properly managed, so here are a few suggestions for parents:

Suggestions
- First **find out what the project entails** and how your child plans to tackle it. Let them know you are there to help.

- Find out **when the project must be completed and handed in, and then help the student to plan a course of action that will enable them to hit the deadline.**
- **Make sure they know** what has to be done and **how marks are allocated to each section of the assignment**.
- If they have any problems, **make sure they talk to the teacher** as early as possible.
- Ensure they have all the **appropriate resources** around them.
- It is pathetic to see a student scratching around at the last minute, trying to finish a project/assignment. This often produces substandard work resulting in a disappointing grade.

Chapter Seven

The Months Leading Up To The Finals

This period is always heavy going for students but, as a parent, there are things you can do to help your child through this demanding session. Always remember the youngster is trying their best to concentrate on their preparation at a time when he or she would rather be doing something else.

Suggestions:
- Help your child **work out a review schedule** and encourage them to stick to it. Have a copy of the review schedule displayed in their study area and another in a place where you can glance at it every day. This is really a continuation of what you should have been doing over the last six years.
- Make sure you have a **quiet place for them to study**, a place where their work can be stored in an organized manner. Organizing their work in a tidy manner makes

for tidy-mindedness, which is reflected in the way they approach their studies.

- **Avoid overburdening the youngster with chores** like taking care of younger siblings. This is where the family can show their support.
- Try to **avoid any arguments** at this time. They are counter-productive and can cause un-necessary stress.
- Point out it **is *not* a good idea to have the TV or radio or any loud music when studying**, although it has been shown that soft, appropriate background music can help.
- Encourage the student to review a topic twice in a session rather than the whole subject.
- The youngster should **plan to cover a subject several times** as the exam approaches. Encourage them to make brief notes as they read. Get them to put the key ideas or points in each topic on cards and use the cards as a review check.
- From time to time, **ask them to explain** to you any topic recently reviewed. If he or she can do this confidently, then there is every chance they will do justice to any question on that topic.
- Make sure **relaxation time is built into review time**. For example, each session could be about thirty minutes, followed by a short break. Regular breaks are essential.
- Encourage the student to ask the teachers for help, if needed.

- Get them to begin each subject by tackling the difficult parts first.
- Very often, working with a friend can help as they can exchange ideas and test each other.
- If he/she is given study-leave, try to be at home whenever you can during this period. This will give you an opportunity to share break-time and have a chat together.
- Encourage the student to work through examination papers from the previous three years. By doing so, they will:

    (a) become **familiar** with the **language** used and some of the ways questions can be phrased.
    (b) get a sense of **timing**, that is, the time he/she ought to spend on each question.
    (c) be able to deal with any gaps in their **knowledge** and be able to brush up on any **skills** in which they may be a bit weak.

Chapter Eight

How To Get The Most Out Of A Parent-Teacher Interview

Apart from feeling vulnerable when crossing the threshold of a school, many parents also feel uncomfortable in the presence of a teacher talking about their children. This usually stems from a lack of confidence. As a result, apart from asking about their child's behavior, many parents end up spending more than 80 percent of the time listening. This is because they lack the relevant knowledge and skills that will enable them to ask the appropriate questions to get the most out of an interview. It is often said that *knowledge is power.* In this context, I would say that a *combination of knowledge and skills* would provide you with the kind of confidence needed to ensure a worthwhile parent-teacher interview. Basically, you have to be prepared. Here are a few suggestions:

Suggestions
    (a) A few weeks before the meeting, get to know what your child is doing in the various courses. Look through their

folders and make written notes of the most recent sets of marks and comments. Also, be sure to read any report or assessment beforehand. This will provide a basis for asking the teacher to explain what is meant by, for example: *fair, fairly good, good, can do better, etc.*

(b) Well in advance, discuss with your child how they are progressing. Try to get a feel for any anxieties they may be having. These are things you can bring to the notice of the teacher. Let your child know that if there are any issues, you would like to hear about them well before the meeting.

With this information, prepare a list of questions along the following lines:

1. Your child's strengths and weaknesses. Find out what can be done to improve where they are weak and what can be done to help them do even better where they are strong.
2. Ask about the kind of resources that will help.
3. Find out how focused he/she is during lessons and whether their work-rate is up to the required standard.
4. Find out if their progress is in line with that expected of the group. If it is below that expected, what can be done to help them improve; if it is above that expected, what can be done to get them to do even better.
5. Ask about the extent to which they participate in classroom discussions and activities.
6. Talk about the youngster's social skills and how well they interact with others, including teachers.

These are just a few ideas on which you can build your discussion. This will give you confidence and enable the kind of interview to take place from which all parties (teacher, parents and child) ought to benefit.

At the interview:
- ***Praise* your child** in front of the teacher for anything well done and try to find out from the teacher why the student did well in those areas of work. This helps to build up your child's confidence.
- Also take the opportunity to *praise the teacher* for the good work they are doing with your child because, like students, teachers thrive on encouragement.
- If the youngster is in the third year of junior high, take the opportunity to discuss the following:

    a) your child's chances of getting on to the courses in which they are interested in doing in senior high.
    (b) the teacher's opinion of your child succeeding in those chosen courses.
    (c) if your child has an idea of what it would like to do after grade twelve, find out from the teacher if the programs they want to follow satisfy college or university requirements. Of course, this should not rule out seeking such advice from the Guidance Department or Student Services.

- It is always a good idea to take a note pad on which to jot down relevant information the teacher may give.

Better still, in order to give you maximum time to listen carefully to what the teacher is saying or for you to ask questions, a small digital recorder could be very handy, *but* please first ask the teacher's permission to use it.

Here are some of the benefits of being prepared for a parent-teacher interview.

1. Your child will see you as **a parent committed to their educational welfare**: one who is willing to do everything it takes to help them navigate their way successfully through a system that may well be strewn with pitfalls and hurdles.
2. The teacher will perceive you as **a parent who is serious** and **committed to your child's schooling,** and not just one paying lip-service to parental involvement, but one prepared to become truly pro-actively engaged.
3. This type of interview has been known to raise the teacher's perception of a family and expectation of the student, all of which can see the teacher going that extra mile to see your child realize their full potential.

It might seem a lot to do, but ask yourself this question: what is the possible outcome if you do not try to get the best return out of a situation in which you are making emotional, physical and financial investment? Since it is possibly the greatest single investment you will ever make, it behooves you to go that extra mile/kilometer to sustain growth in your investment. By doing this, the chances are your child will become more confident and willing to do their best and the teacher willing to do that bit extra to help your child. **Always bear in mind that while the teacher expects you to listen to what they have to say, they also expect you to ask questions, but you must be prepared.**

Chapter Nine

Homework Scenarios And Some Suggestions For Parents

Children tend to fall into two broad categories with regard to homework:

(a) those who are keen to get on and who will do their best to do their homework without having to be constantly pursued by their parents and teachers.
(b) those who see it as a chore to be got rid of as quickly as possible, who pay little or no attention to the quality and who may often find any excuse to get out of it.

Schools differ in the amount of emphasis placed on homework, but it can be generally accepted that in most high schools, it is emphasized and well structured.

Here are four scenarios to help you as parents:
<u>Scenario one</u>: *Doing homework before parents arrive home in the evening.*

David arrives home from school at his usual time but well before his parents. He gets himself a drink or perhaps a snack.

(a) He may then decide to start his homework and try to get most or all of it done and neatly presented before dinner or

(b) He may hurry it through in order to play games or go outside with friends, particularly during the summer months.

Mum or Dad arrives home to find David playing games, watching TV or outside with his friends.

"David, have you done your homework yet?' 'Yes mum,' continuing on his cell phone or iPad, game or simply watching TV. As a parent, you have a choice: you can either *accept* what he said or *question* what he said. My suggestion is to adopt the latter approach. After you have settled and probably after supper, **question what he said**.

Suggestions

- **Ask to see it**. Check that it satisfies the requirements and is neatly presented. Make sure it checks out with what is written in his journal.
- Get him to **tell you something about it**. Find out if he understands it. If he cannot describe what he has done in a sensible manner to you, then he did not understand it.
- If he does not understand it, **help him if you can**. If you cannot, make a point of asking the teacher to explain it

again to your child. The alternative is to call on an older sibling who can help, or a friend.
- Do not let such a situation go unattended, because to do so, you would be **reducing their chances of fully understanding the subject**. There would be a gap in their knowledge.
- If he/she has not done their homework, then it is your duty to see **that it is done**. If you think the reason given for not doing it is unacceptable, then consider withdrawing one of their privileges.
- It tells the child you are interested in and serious about what they are doing and that he/she ought to be serious as well.

Scenario Two: *I don't have any homework tonight*

Never accept this blindly. David could decide he does not want to be bothered with any work tonight because he has other things to do. To make this convincing, he may even decide not to write the homework in his journal, so that when you ask to see his journal, you will see no entry has been made for that day and assume none was set.

Suggestions
- Ask to see his journal. (Refer to the copy of his homework timetable that you should have pinned up in an appropriate place.)
- If homework has not been given when it ought to be, **get in touch with the teacher** concerned as soon as

possible and get an explanation. *Never accept that given by your child.*

- If homework was set but David opted not to do it, then, as a parent, you must make sure it is done, for the same reasons stated above. **Under no account must he be allowed to get away with it.** If he gets away with it once, he will try it again and again until the practice becomes a habit and then the habit becomes part of his character. I am sure I don't have to tell you the likely outcome.

- If this situation arises too frequently in any given subject, alarm bells should start to ring. It is time to **pay a visit to the school by appointment** because it is essential you find out what is going on. Here are a few possible explanations:

    a) Your child might have been sent out of the lesson and therefore was absent when the homework was given. (*discipline problem!!*)
    b) A rift might be developing between them and the teacher, making it impossible for teaching to take place when your child is in the classroom. In other words, he/she is seen as a general nuisance.
    c) Your child might not have the confidence to tell the teacher he/she does not quite understand the topic. If this is so, they may see it as pointless in doing any homework.

d) The teacher may have a good reason for not setting homework on that day, or he/she might have been absent on that day.
e) It might be a sign that the your child is beginning to show disaffection not only with the teacher, but perhaps with school in general, or other undesirable influences are probably beginning to take hold.

Whatever the reason, early diagnosis will allow time for something to be done.

Scenario Three: *I did it at school*

This is the kind of scenario that tends to appear in the second year at junior high. If, when asked, the child replies by saying, 'I did it at school,' you ought to adopt the following approach.

Suggestions

- As soon as possible, preferably the next day, get in touch with the subject teacher/s to find out if it was handed in and whether it was of an acceptable standard.
- Make sure you see that piece of homework as soon as possible. Again, check for presentation. Remember, you don't necessarily have to know the subject. You are merely looking for presentation and quality, for the way the child thinks is often expressed in the manner in which they present their classwork and homework.

- It is advisable to encourage your child not to do homework at school except where supervised by a teacher.
- Doing it at home gives you an opportunity to discuss it and to find out their strengths and weaknesses.

Scenario Four: *Doing homework after supper*

It ought to be agreed between you and your child when homework is to be started. Do not leave anything to chance. If homework should start at seven, then seven it has to be every evening, except when something happens that makes it impossible. This is a way of teaching them to *plan their work and work their plan.*

Here are some advantages of doing homework after supper:
a) The child has had time to relax and, having had supper, is now more physically and hopefully mentally ready to do homework.
b) It is always a good idea to set a good example by making a little sacrifice. Instead of settling down to TV yourself, sacrifice an hour and sit with them as they do their work. This is crucial during the years at junior high. Try to be in the same room. You may choose to read a novel, or a newspaper, or better still, as some parents do, start some kind of distance learning course however simple, whereby you can do your homework while they are doing theirs. **This is called leading from the front by example.** Indeed, is this too much to ask in the interest of a child in whom you are making emotional, financial and physical investment?

c) Being in the same room means you are there to answer any questions and give help where you can. It also encourages a kind of rapport that tells the child *you are there to support them* and that you are interested in what they are doing.

The first three scenarios tend to arise more frequently with students in junior high. By the time they reach grade ten, they ought to be well-grounded into an acceptable approach to homework, but you must still be vigilant right up to grade twelve.

Remember that how you respond to the answers given in the first three situations tells your child how serious you are about their education. If the youngster is trying to play the school off against the parent, it must be demonstrated that you and the school are on the same path and that the only thing to do, if he/she wants to get on, is to do what is expected of them. They must never be allowed to think they can play one off against the other. This, of course, is the approach to adopt from grade seven. It helps the student to develop a sense of responsibility, a sense of direction and purpose, as well as better time-management: characteristics they will need throughout school and beyond.

CHAPTER TEN

HELPING YOUR CHILD COPE WITH THE STRESS OF HOMEWORK

Homework can cause a student much stress, and if not properly managed, can also cause much stress to a parent, sometimes resulting in parent-child conflict. Seen from this perspective, it is a challenge to both parent and child. Always make time to talk to your child about their homework. By doing so, they will see you as a **source of strength and encouragement**. What follows are a few tips to enable both parties to better cope with such a challenge.

Suggestions
The **first** concerns helping your child to start their assignment/ homework.
- If it seems the student is finding it difficult to make a start, advise them to begin with the easiest task. This may well be the one they like most. This done, the momentum will be carried over to the harder task.

- However, if you think your child is capable or has the drive to tackle the more difficult assignment first, encourage them to do so early in the process.
- You must always bear in mind also that what you may perceive as the best approach for your child may not be so for them. Your duty is to help them make that decision.

The **second** thing is for you to find out what particular task your child would prefer to do at any given time. For instance:

- Would they like to do a task involving problem solving like, for example, mathematics or science, or would they feel more comfortable doing an assignment that requires a lot of reading like, for example, reading a novel or writing an essay?
- Perhaps the youngster might feel better tackling the kind of homework that involves memorizing like, for example, history, geography or social studies.
- The reason for this is that since each of the above requires a particular method of thinking and focus, your duty as a parent is to help the child decide on the kind of study that will be most productive at that time. This is extremely important, as much time can be wasted and frustration can set in attempting a task for which the child has neither the drive nor energy to do.

Thirdly, from time-to-time, encourage your child to change where they sit to do their homework. Research has shown that simply alternating the place in the room, or even the room itself, can improve retention.

Finally, when studying for a test or exam, it is also a good idea to encourage him or her to vary how and where the material is learned. Students resort to various methods. For instance:

- Some like to sing the facts as they learn them.
- Some like to say the information aloud.
- Some like to walk around.
- Others like to find a spot far removed.
- As for me, as a lad in the Caribbean, I would find a suitable tree about 200 meters away from home. I would make myself comfortable in the fork between a large branch and the trunk and do my reading and memory work.
- Always remember, you do not necessarily have to know how to do the assignment to help your child, but by talking to them about the subject/s they are doing you will gain a better understanding and be in a better position to help. Just think how the youngster will feel if you ask them: *Do you have a lot of homework tonight? If so, let's see how I can help.* Always remember that being there when they are doing their homework will help them stay motivated.

CHAPTER ELEVEN

CLASS WORK, HOMEWORK AND TEACHER EXPECTATION

Perception is the way the teacher sees your child, what that teacher thinks of your child. Most teachers get it right in that they paint a fairly accurate picture of the child and their ability level based on previous records. Unfortunately, there will be some who may get it wrong from time to time. The is significant in that the teacher's perception will shape their expectations of your child.

Expectations denote what a teacher believes a student can do. Generally, the more a teacher believes a student can do, the higher the achievement of the student. Likewise, the less a teacher believes a child can do, the lower the achievement is likely to be.

Responses to a teacher's perception and expectation of a child are often shown in the way that child pursues their goal, the skills they are prepared to engage and the energy they are prepared to use, as well as the level of rewards they expect from their effort.

Outcome is the end product brought about by the above. A teacher's high expectations of a child brings about a high level of interaction and attention from the teacher. This enables the student to have a high expectation of themselves and encourages the child to give of their best and gain the expected achievement level, which is usually high. The reverse is also true, namely, low teacher expectation can be reflected in a child having a low expectation of themselves, resulting in a low achievement level.

Since perceptions of children's intellectual ability can affect the goals they set, then teachers (and to some extent parents) who underestimate children's potential will tend to set goals that are low.

Suggestions

How to get a general idea of a teacher's perception and expectation of your child.

1. Keep a close eye on the level of work done in the classroom and given as homework. If the child and you feel that it is well below their level of ability, it is worthy of investigation. Have a polite discussion with the teacher concerned.
2. Pay attention to the level of marks given and any written comments made on any assignment or piece of homework. This can often tell you the quality of work the teacher is prepared to accept. If you think

such a mark or comment does not reflect the quality of work presented, then it is worth investigating. This is especially so if you feel that a piece of work has been over-rated. If this is so, it shows the teacher may be prepared to accept anything from your child. The child suffers. Fortunately, the great majority of teachers are professionals who go about their job with the greatest of diligence.
3. Be vigilant at all times. Keep talking to your child. If he or she complains of boredom in lessons, it might be that the level of work given is too low. The youngster is in need of more challenging work. It is time to pay a visit to the school.

This is extremely significant, as a teacher's perception of a student can often enhance or frustrate that student's chances of success. A teacher's perception and expectation can set a high or low ceiling of achievement for a child. Low teacher expectation can bring about low student- expectation and under-achievement. This may result in boredom, a desire to give up (drop out), or failing to register a satisfactory grade in the Certificate of Achievement and/or High School diploma. By contrast, high teacher expectation can see work set that is challenging which, together with teacher encouragement, often produces a student that is highly motivated and keen to do their best.

Chapter Twelve

Parenting Style And Classroom Practice

The primary reason, apart from the legal one, why parents send children to school is to learn and develop in a manner that will make them desirable citizens. Since in most schools much learning takes place in a classroom setting, it is reasonable to expect a certain code of behavior to exist if learning is to take place. Students are expected to follow a set of guidelines laid down by the school and implemented by the teacher in his/her management of the classroom. It is their duty to ensure that their classroom management and practice produce the kind of environment conducive to learning. Research suggests that, where good classroom practice and parenting style support each other, excellent results tend to follow.

Briefly, there are three main types of parenting style:

> The *authoritarian* style in which the child does as told. There is no discussion, no dialogue. Such

children generally tend to grow up lacking confidence and are less likely to take part in classroom discussions. That is not to say they don't often do very well.

The permissive or non-directive style. This is where children are allowed to grow and develop in a liberal environment. It is the 'free-discipline' approach. Some writers refer to it as 'indulgent,' in that parents tend to indulge children by responding to their every demand in an effort to avoid confrontation. This they do without themselves making demands.

The *authoritative style,* which lies midway between the two extremes described above. In this, the parent retains control, but listens to and discusses matters with the child. This is the style that reflects most closely the kind of classroom practice found in successful schools.

As a parent, it is your responsibility to find out as much as you can about how teachers in charge of your child manage their classrooms. Although there will be differences between teachers in the way they do so, you will find that in successful schools there is a core of principles and values which govern and inform that practice. Your role here is to find out the extent to which your parenting style supports good classroom practice and, if necessary, to adapt to make it easier for your child at school. This avoids the child having to deal with conflicting messages from you and the teacher.

Suggestions
- **Find out** if it is necessary to modify your parenting style in any way to make it easier for your child, because the home and the school ought to be singing from the same sheet if the child is to make appreciable progress.
- **Encourage** your child to ask questions and to engage in conversation with you. This helps them to develop an inquiring mind and to build confidence, qualities they need in school and after.
- Get into the habit of **listening carefully** to what your child has to say. Respect their opinion and if you have to differ, try to express this in a manner that will not destroy their confidence.
- When there is a misunderstanding within the immediate family, try to solve it **through negotiation** rather than confrontation. Remember, patterns of behavior seen and heard at home are taken to school. Children learn by example, so be sure the pattern of behavior displayed at home is the one you are happy to have exhibited at school: one that will enhance your child's chances of success at school.
- Make sure that any chores your child is expected to carry out at home are **well-done**, like tidying their room on a regular basis. Do not accept substandard work. By ensuring that whatever the youngster is told to do is done to the very best helps him or her to develop

'tidy-mindedness' and a sense of responsibility, all of which is reflected in the manner in which they approach school work and interact with others.
- **Impress on your child** how important it is to listen carefully to instructions and carry them out. This helps them to concentrate. Moreover, teachers tend to be attracted to students who listen and make an effort to indulge in constructive conversation.
- Try to point out that there is nothing to be gained by being anti-authority. Not many teachers will tolerate such an attitude. Most teachers see it as disruptive behavior, which generally results in the child being asked to leave the classroom. Who suffers?
- Always keep lines of communication between yourself and your child open. They must feel you are approachable at all times and about any matter.
- This is not meant to dictate to you as a parent how you ought to conduct your lives. Instead, they are merely suggestions, which I hope you will take on board in your effort to help your child through high school successfully.

CHAPTER THIRTEEN

HELPING YOUR CHILD MAKE DECISIONS

As parents, we are constantly making decisions, both minor and major. Children, too, are always making decisions. Since making choices is really a matter of decision-making, I want to spend a little time on *how we can help children to make decisions* as a foundation on which to choose friends, courses and programs.

Children need to know the mechanics of decision-making. For example, a teenager will have a hard time choosing a career if they have never explored the options. Likewise, they will have a hard time making good financial decisions if he/she has not been taught the principles of money-management.

A student may have difficulty in deciding what programs/courses to follow, but if they have been taught well, they will be able to make choices based on their future career plans, their interests, their ability and the work-load involved. But even if a child knows all the processes in decision making, they will not learn to make good decisions unless they are given the opportunity to make some. We can therefore be of great help to our children by allowing them to make decisions when they are ready, even although it is not always easy to tell when a child is ready to do so.

Suggestions
- Get into the habit of allowing your child to make decisions in areas of little consequence, for example: the arrangement of their room or what they like for lunch. It will not hurt if it turns out that they don't like the arrangement of the room or dislike the lunch pack. This would at least teach them to put a little more thought into their choices and to consider the outcome more carefully.
- At this stage it is always better to give them a limited choice, for having some successful decisions where the choices are limited will help them develop confidence in their decision-making skills. From here, they can make more responsible decisions, like the clothes they buy.
- Sometimes children avoid making decisions because they do not want to be responsible for a wrong outcome. They would rather have you decide and then blame you if it turns out to be wrong. But just because children might not want to make decisions doesn't mean they can't.
- Children who grow up making their own decisions (of course, within a set of boundaries) become responsible adults. A parent once asked his son why he was often approached by other boys for help in solving problems.

Since I was very young you forced me to make decisions: choose my own clothes, arrange my own furniture, to spend my own money. Did you like it? asked his dad. *No, I hated it, but I did learn how to decide.*

- Although you should allow children to make decisions, you should not withdraw your advice because quite often, as parents, you can give a child needed insight that will help in the decision they have to make. At times, we can all benefit from sharing our ideas and feelings with another person, and often another person's perception can give us information needed to make a wise choice. Therefore, as parents, we should not deny our children that help.
- Although parents can and should advise children if necessary, once a child has made a decision, you should let that child experience the consequences. Be willing to let the child make a mistake, particularly if that mistake will not hurt him/her forever. For example, if your child, knowing a piece of school work, perhaps an essay, was due to be handed in several weeks or days ago, suddenly comes to you in tears the night before for help, it would not help that child if you did the essay, or called the teacher to ask for more time. If you did that, you would be denying the child that opportunity to learn from their mistakes.
- There is a tendency for parents to shield children from every possibility of failure, but in doing so, they deny them an important factor in their success. If a child is never allowed to fail and every mistake is treated for

them, they will be in for a rude awakening later. But that must not be seen as passivity, for failure to act on bad behavior will teach children that there are no boundaries and no consequences for violating them.

- If, however, you feel a child is making a decision that does not go well with those *values* held by the family, then it might not be wise to give them a choice in such matters. This is why many teenagers who are quite capable and desirous of making certain decisions still need *family values* as a reserve support when they are faced with, for example, undesirable peer pressure. It is our duty as parents, therefore, not to let them down when they need us. Always remember that what your child needs mostly from you is your confidence in them. Some parents are too quick to dismiss a child's potential and dismiss their dreams. In the final analysis, you may be the only one who believes in your child, but if that child knows they have your support, they will make you proud with their choices.
- As children grow older and are more capable of making important decisions, we ought to include them in many of the policy decisions that will affect their lives. For example, how late they are allowed to stay out, or the kind of parties they will attend. This tells them that we respect their decisions and their right to set the course for their lives. It also gives them a forum to openly discuss problems for which they may need and desire our advice.

Here are four basic steps in the mechanics of decision-making you may find useful to teach them:

Define the problem: What is the decision you need to make? What is the problem it solves?

Explore the options: To solve the problem, what options do I have? Are the options possible? Are they safe or risky? Are there lots of "what if" questions like, "What if I fail?" Make sure he/she understands the consequences. Each option has pluses and minuses, and some choices cost more than others. Some options may have immediate benefits, while for others, benefits may be delayed. Thinking through the consequences of each option will help children narrow down the range of acceptable choices.

Make a decision: When there are different options, your child must choose one and implement it. Putting off a decision without a very good reason is mere indecisiveness and does not help.

Evaluate and learn from the decision: Once the decision is made and acted on, find out what you can learn from it. If it was the best decision, look at how it was made and let it become a pattern. If it was the wrong decision, look at the processes and see what the child missed.

Remember to teach by example. Model your own best decision-making skills so that your child can observe and learn. Be there before he/she decides. While they are younger, be around enough to help them think things through before making a decision. Talking them through the process in advance is helpful. But always remember that they will learn more from trial and error than by you making every decision for them. Having strong problem-solving and decision-making skills will help them know what they need to become a strong decision maker in later life.

CHAPTER FOURTEEN

How To Help Your Child Using Motivation

Schooling today can be very demanding and stressful on both children and parents, but there are strategies that will enable you and your child to cope while enhancing that child's performance. Motivation is one such strategy. I hope you will find the following tips useful.

Suggestions

Try to **have a positive attitude towards school**. Base your conversations about school on what the child is doing well, rather than what they aren't doing well. This is not to say you must overlook what is not done well. Find out what is their best time of the school day and talk about it. Ask about the activities they enjoy. This shows you care. You may learn more about them than you think, for example, things that bother them as well as things they find challenging or frustrating. Speak in a positive tone and avoid nagging and long lectures.

Try setting goals with your child: goals that are high but achievable. Your child will be more motivated to do their best if he/she is working toward a result that is meaningful and important to them. Do bear in mind, however, that this only works if the goals represent what your child wants to do. Talk with them to make sure their goals are in line with family values. Here are a few tips:

- Help your child set a goal that represents what they want to accomplish but it must be a specific goal. For instance, instead of saying, "I want to do better in science," why not say, 'I want to get a grade B in science by the end of the year."
- Help them plan the steps they have to take to reach that target. .Make sure they include times and dates for completing each step as well as time for any extra activity. For instance, if they have hockey-practice two or three times a week, they may have to build into their plan some time for extra homework perhaps on weekends.

Have the goals posted in a place where they can be referred to often, at least once a week. This will give them a chance to review the goals and make any necessary amendments.
Sustained practice in something can be beneficial. For instance, have a chat with their teacher about their progress. If they are behind in a particular subject, encourage them to do an extra fifteen minutes each day. If their reading level is below that expected, ask the teacher to suggest some titles

that will help. Make sure they read at the current level rather than above. Becoming good reading at that level will give them the momentum to move to a higher level.

Recognize and celebrate even small successes. Children, especially the younger ones, can find it difficult grasping long-term rewards. As a parent, you must acknowledge any small successes your child has. Avoid telling them they haven't done well enough. Instead, build in rewards for short-term goals. You must however avoid giving cash and gifts for every week that homework is finished on time or for doing well in a test. This will soon cease to be effective. Rewards can take the form of time spent together. You may be surprised to learn how much of a reward your child might consider a day alone fishing with dad or a movie out with mum.

Always bear in mind that **your child's success is the result of the combined effort of a team:** you the parent, the teacher and the child, and that you must therefore be engaged. It is no time for the 'blame game.' Instead, it is time to work constructively with teachers and your child.

Teach your child to learn not just from their failures but from their successes. Not doing well with some areas of schoolwork is not the end of the world. Teach your child that it's okay to feel a little down or disappointed, but that they can often learn a lot from their successes. For instance, if they did well in a recent test or exam, congratulate them, but also get them to look at what they did to achieve such a good result and get them to transfer that approach to other studies.

Chapter Fifteen
How Family Values Can Influence Schooling

The chances that the suggestions made in the foregoing pages will be implemented will depend largely on where education is positioned in the order of things within the family values. The value placed on education by a family will largely determine the amount of investment a parent is prepared to make in a child's schooling. Family values reflect who we are, our culture and our own unique heritage. When we are clear about our values, we are better able to establish priorities and make decisions we can live with and by. Such values encompass those things we learn from our families in childhood that build our character: those things that build personal growth and education, while offering love and protection. *Values influence the choices we make; they shape what we believe and how we perceive things; values are a part of our experience that affects our behavior. They encompass our attitudes and the standards we set for our actions and beliefs. They also tell others what is important to us and guide our decision making.*

For instance, we use our resources – time, money and brain power – on the things we value.

Here are some reasons why you, as a parent, ought to identify and communicate family values to your children. By doing so,

- ***it helps them in making personal decisions***, like, for example, when choosing peer friends, program/course choices, or whether to do or not to do well at school.

- ***it helps them manage time, energy and resources,*** like for example, knowing how to strike the right balance between academic and non-academic activities; how to find the right person/s when in need of help.

- ***it enables them to know themselves better***, for example, helping them to recognize and, hopefully, understand where they and the family stand on the socio-economic landscape and perhaps the part they themselves must play in the family.

- ***it also helps to eliminate some of the confusions in life***, like for example, those brought about by the conflicting demands made on them by different expectations of parents, school and peer friends, as well as their own. Much as your child would like to satisfy all, they cannot do so and therefore have to make appropriate choices. Such decisions will largely be dependent on how well steeped they may be in family values.

- ***it brings about a better understanding and respect for others who have different values.*** This especially applies to their interaction with those of other ethnic groups.

Children need to know how to act and how not to act. They need to have clear instructions, not conflicting messages from family members and others in their lives. Always remember that through the many interactions between school-age children and others around them, the child learns what is acceptable, and what is not. Much of what they value will be played out in the classroom, on the playground and through interactions with peers and adults, including teachers.

Goals and decisions are made based upon influential people (like parents) in their lives, but because peers tend to become a very strong force during the adolescent period, strong positive values are therefore critical in helping the youngster to make positive choices that bring positive results.

Because children will always be the future for a better tomorrow, it is our duty to provide them with the necessary tools that will enable them to know what is correct and what is wrong. We must also understand that our actions deliver the clearest meanings. For example, the way we spend our free time, or even the way we spend our money will be reflected in children's character. We therefore have to set rules that reflect the values we believe in and practice, because the meaning of the values will be easier for children to understand.

As parents, we ought to promote the self-esteem of our children because, by doing so, we make them feel competent and capable. The challenge we therefore have is to encourage independence but also provide boundaries and rules to help them develop the ability to know what they need and what they have to do to achieve it.

CHAPTER SIXTEEN

SOME TIPS ON HOW TO DEAL WITH PARENT-CHILD CONFLICT

As children grow, conflict is inevitable. You must bear in mind that, as a young adolescent, your child will be trying increasingly to assert their autonomy.

Suggestions
- Try to **deal with a conflict as soon as it arises**. If you do not know what to do or say, acknowledge the problem and say, "We will talk about this later." The child then knows you are not letting the situation slip or go un-noticed. It also gives you time to seek help and advice if necessary.
- Be sure to **listen carefully** to what your child has to say. Give them a chance to be heard and you must *really listen*.
- Make sure you are quite clear about what behaviors are and are not acceptable. Conflicts often occur when children work out that you are unclear about these

boundaries. Practitioners agree that the most effective parenting style is one that has clear rules but also **listens to and values the child's opinions and ideas**.
- **Try talking to other parents** about the conflicts you are having. You might find there are others struggling with a similar situation and, by discovering you are not the only one, can help to give you the confidence to work through the problem.
- Make an effort to handle any family disagreement in a manner that allows your child to see you as a positive parental role model. Let them see you in action and learn.

Chapter Seventeen

How To Be A Positive Parental Role Model

For a youngster, a positive role model can provide them with an example of their potential by affirming their dreams of who they can be. He or she can be inspired to be the best they can be. It is easy for children to be swayed by many influences in society, but having a good role model whom they think is cool, or who thinks they are cool, makes it easier to avoid unhealthy influences and stay focused on what they could be.

Why a parent is perhaps the best role model
- Research has shown that having a positive role model and in particular an individual known to the child, for example a parent, has been associated with higher self-esteem and higher grades.
- Always remember the most important persons in a child's life are their parents: they are the first and most important teachers.

- Because of the innate trust children have in parents, they feel anything parents do is the true and proper way to behave.
- Children learn more from what they see and hear around them than from what they are told.
- You have more influence over your child than you probably realize, which is why children tend to pattern their behavior after you, the parent.
- By becoming a positive role model, you can become a good mentor. My research suggests that many children are more comfortable with the informal method of mentoring, which largely involves parents, than the more formal type imposed at school. It is the kind of informal support that allows parents to become more aware of any significant changes in the child, giving them the chance to vary the type and degree of attention, help, advice, information and encouragement.

Suggestions

- As a parent, you have to **provide the kind of family values** on which your child can draw when under attack from external unhealthy influences.
- **Think about the parenting style you use in the family**. Is it confrontational or is it one based on listening and reasoning? Is it dictatorial or is it one that allows the youngster to have a say?
- One of the best things about having parents as role models is that they are within easy reach. It is your

duty, therefore, to **make sure you are always accessible for advice, help and support**.
- **Display patterns of behavior** you would expect your child to have if he/she is to progress through school with the minimum of difficulty. Lead from the front by example.
- Give them the kind of **inspiration and encouragement,** particularly when things appear to be difficult.
- Try to **understand the stress** the child might be experiencing, particularly after fourteen, due to competing expectations all making their demands on them: parental, teacher, peer-group and their own expectations. Whom should they seek to satisfy?
- Be one who is ready to **listen** before taking a stand. Show this through sustained conversation and keeping lines of communication open.
- Give them the kind of **confidence** and feeling of **security** in the knowledge that, whatever the outcome, they always have your full support.

BIBLIOGRAPHY

Alleyne D, EdD (2010) Rules of engagement: An in-depth study of the educational encounters of a group of academically successful African-Caribbean boys and their families across five UK schools.

BBC-Health (2011): Starting Secondary School.

Cameron L (1997): Improving Parent-teacher interviews.

Ellerby & Daymond (2005): The parent guide to secondary school.

Ensign (1978 April, p.18)

Gov. of Alberta (2012): My Child's Learning, A Parent Resource.

Measer & Fleetham (2005): Moving to secondary school.

Niz S (2013): How to do things.

Williams A (1997): Intergenerational Equity.

CPSIA information can be obtained at www.ICGtesting.com
Printed in the USA
LVOW02s2349240315

431772LV00005B/11/P